S0-DJQ-104

Report Factory

by Murray Suid and Wanda Lincoln • illustrated by Mike Artell

Publisher: Roberta Suid
Editor: Carol Whiteley
Production: Susan Pinkerton

Related writing books from Monday Morning Books, Inc: *Book Factory, Writing Hangups, Greeting Cards, Write Through the Year, For the Love of Editing, For the Love of Letter Writing, For the Love of Research, For the Love of Stories.*

monday morning®

Monday Morning is a registered trademark of
Monday Morning Books, Inc.

Entire contents copyright ©1991 by Monday Morning
Books, Inc., Box 1680, Palo Alto, California 94302

Permission is hereby granted to the individual purchaser to reproduce
student materials in this book for non-commercial individual or classroom
use only. Permission is not granted for school-wide, or system-wide,
reproduction of materials.

ISBN 1-878279-17-3

Printed in the United States of America
9 8 7 6 5 4 3 2 1

CONTENTS

INTRODUCTION

The word *report* means literally "to carry back." The reporter's job consists of finding and sharing information about people, places, things, or ideas.

These days, information can be presented in many ways such as books, press conferences, radio and TV programs, and even board games. The *Report Factory* aims to help you bring this kind of authentic, *whole learning* excitement into your room, helping you to:

- integrate language arts with the entire curriculum
- introduce students to the challenges of researching
- create interest in a variety of topics
- develop questioning and thinking skills
- acknowledge—and make use of—different learning styles
- foster independent learning

USING THE BOOK

The *Report Factory* is divided into four parts:

- Research Practices gives activities that help students learn how to gather facts for their reports. This section identifies the three main processes all reporters must know about: reading, interviewing, and eyewitness observing. If your students are already skillful researchers, then you may wish to turn directly to the Projects section.

- Projects—by far the largest part of the book— offers step-by-step duplicatable directions for creating dozens of innovative and traditional reports—*all based on real-world models*. Many of these activities are accompanied by bonus lists of topics that can spark hundreds of original—not copied—projects.

  Of course, no teacher can use all these options. Choose those that fit your overall program and that interest you and your students.

- Tools of the Trade offers mini-lessons on getting the most from the devices mentioned in the Projects section: overhead projector, tape recorder, still and video cameras, photocopy machine, and computer.

- Managing the Report Factory outlines a method for guiding students from the first step of a project (getting an idea) to the finale (self-evaluation). Duplicatable progress forms simplify the task of tracking student achievements.

A final page—Whole Learning Is News—presents an article that documents and celebrates this type of integrated, curiosity-based learning. We wish you the same kind of success in your teaching.

Research Practices

Many students dread report writing because they really don't understand it. They think research means copying from a book, and no one wants to be a copycat.

In fact, copying is no more appropriate for report writing than it is for poetry or story writing. An authentic report in large part is a creative work. The following practices are meant to help students become creative researchers.

NO COPYING

PRACTICE 1. ASKING QUESTIONS

For students to become creative researchers, they must learn that research begins with questions, not facts. Facts are gathered only to answer the reporter's questions.

Teach the different levels of questions:
- A. Fact questions such as "What does that weigh?"
- B. Process questions such as "How was that made?"
- C. Value questions such as "Which is more valuable—this painting or that one, and why?"
- D. Speculative questions such as "What would happen if . . . ?"

Then, on a regular basis (daily, if possible), give students an opportunity to brainstorm questions—all sorts of questions. Hold up an object and have students write as many questions about it as they can. Sometimes arrange for this brainstorming to be done in groups.

Also, have students read nonfiction pieces—newspaper and magazine articles, chapters from books—and list questions that they see are answered in the text.

As a journal activity, have students write questions that occur to them in the course of their daily activities.

PRACTICE 2. LOCATING INFORMATION

One reason students find research boring is that they frequently use only one of the three major ways to collect information. This would be like eating only one type of food—say, just milk products—rather than a balanced diet.

Experienced researchers collect their facts in three ways:

    A. by reading books, newspapers, and other materials

    B. by interviewing experts

    C. by observing firsthand (seeing, hearing, etc.)

Most reporters use at least two sources when working on a project. For example, a reporter investigating how the zoo cares for its new elephant may watch the elephant in its enclosure and also ask the elephant keeper a series of questions.

A fun way to prepare students for using all three sources is to send them off on information scavenger hunts. All that's required is a "facts-to-find list" (see examples below). Some lists should concentrate on just one source—say, books or people. Others can combine sources.

When students return from their hunts, they should share their experiences. *Hint:* After taking part in a few teacher-made scavenger hunts, students may wish to create their own challenges for their classmates—and even for the teacher.

Sample Scavenger Hunt Fact Lists

Print-Only Information Hunt

1. Find three books that give information about the Earl of Sandwich.
2. Find a book that lists the zip code of the White House.
3. Find two books that have maps of the Province of Ontario, Canada.
4. Find a magazine article that has information about women inventors.
5. Find a book or an article that was written by someone who has walked on the moon.

People-Only Scavenger Hunt

1. Find someone who was born before 1945.
2. Find someone who is a twin or who is friends with a twin.
3. Find someone who has seen a rocket blast off firsthand (not on TV).

4. Find someone who knows how to juggle.
5. Find someone who loves opera.
6. Find someone who has ridden on a camel.

Observation Scavenger Hunt

Study a dollar bill and answer the following questions:

1. How many times does the word "one" appear?
2. What is the least number of 1's that can appear?
3. What direction is Washington facing?
4. Whose signature appears on the bill?
5. How big (in inches or centimeters) is the bill?
6. What are three ways that the front and the back are alike?
7. What are three ways that the front and the back are different?

PRACTICE 3. PARAPHRASING

Most students do not feel comfortable taking notes from a book. This is because they do not have a method for putting text into their own words. Before sending them out in the quest for facts, it makes sense to teach them how to paraphrase.

Give students a short piece of about 100 words. Allow them to write down ten words or brief phrases meant to help them recall the important information. They should then put the reading aside, and write their own versions based on their notes. When they are finished, have them compare their versions with a partner and then with the original article. Encourage them to discuss the differences.

By working from notes rather than from the original, the students are forced to put the information into their own words. And this, in fact, is what most experienced writers do.

Of course, like all important skills, paraphrasing can't be learned in a day. This exercise should be frequently repeated.

REPORT PROJECTS

BOARD GAMES

Creating a board game gives the game maker a chance to entertain people while teaching them all sorts of facts.

DIRECTIONS:
1. Choose a subject for the game—a person, place, thing, or activity. Don't overlook topics of local interest, for example, the school or the community.
2. Using research, compose a list of facts about the subject.
3. Decide how the game will be played. *Hint:* It's often possible to invent a new game by making changes in an old game such as Monopoly or Trivial Pursuit.
4. Sketch the board, showing places that players will visit during the game. For example, in a game about blood circulation, players might land on the heart, the lungs, the brain, the kidneys, the bones, and so on.
5. Create the board, pieces to move, and any other needed components. For example, if players have to answer questions, make up question and answer cards.
6. Write the rules.
7. Test the game. Is it interesting? Are the rules clear? Did the players learn anything? If necessary, make changes and try it again.
8. Try selling copies as a fund-raising project.

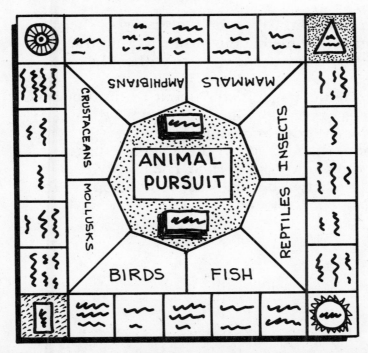

BOOKS

Scientists, explorers, inventors, historians, and other experts often need the space of a whole book to fully report on what they have learned.

DIRECTIONS:

1. Decide who will write the book—one person? a group?—and then choose an idea.

2. Do a bit of preliminary research to make sure that there is enough information for a book.

3. Plan the look of the book. How big will the pages be? Will some pages have just words? Will some have just pictures? Will some have pictures and words?

4. Estimate the number of pages. Knowing the length will help determine how much research to do.

5. Break the main subject into chapter topics. For example, a book about airplanes might include chapters about the frame, the motors, the controls, and so on.

6. Carry out the detailed research for each chapter.

7. Write the text. *Hint:* It's usually a good idea to follow the same pattern for all chapters. For example, each chapter might begin with a brief, true story or with an amazing fact, and then end with a list of think-about-it questions.

8. Add illustrations. These can be drawings, photographs, maps, diagrams, and so on.

9. Write an introduction. Give a brief overview of the subject, explain why someone might like to read the book, and describe the process used to gather the information.

10. Include a contents page, a note about the author or authors, an index, a glossary, and a reading list.

11. Put the pages in order and number them.

12. To make more than one copy, duplicate the pages and then bind them into books. *Hint:* The library may welcome these nonfiction books. Also, send a copy to the local newspaper's book reviewer.

BOX REPORTS

Sometimes the best way to teach a subject is to let people see—and touch—things for themselves.

DIRECTIONS:
1. Choose a report topic that people can learn about by handling inexpensive objects, for example, bicycle gears, bones, candles, cloth, crystals, leaves, rocks, rubbings, seeds, tools, and wood.
2. Do research about the objects.
3. Write facts about each object on index cards, sheets of paper, or pieces of cardboard.
4. Protect fragile objects. For example, laminate leaves on pieces of cardboard.
5. Use string or glue to attach each item to its writeup. *Option:* Write all the facts on a separate sheet and refer to the objects by number.
6. Place all the items in a box.
7. Write an introduction that tells what is inside the box and what the readers can learn by studying the objects. Include tips on how to handle the materials. End with a reminder to return all items to the box.
8. Glue, tape, or staple the introduction to the outside of the box. Use a colorful headline that will draw readers' attention to the introduction.

Variation: To do a box report about large objects—for example, trucks or elephants—use models.

BULLETIN BOARDS

Student-made bulletin boards add zest to a room or hall and give the creators a tremendous sense of pride.

DIRECTIONS:
1. After researching a topic, decide what job the bulletin board is to do. Choices include:
- giving information
- teaching a skill
- displaying things
- getting readers to do something, such as writing a letter to the mayor

2. Decide whether people will simply read the board or get involved with it, for example, by adding an opinion to a survey sheet attached to the board.

3. List the kinds of materials that will appear on the board, for example, words, drawings, photographs, and objects such as labels from tin cans.

4. Sketch a layout. This will show the positions of the headline, the art or objects, the captions, and so on.

5. Collect the needed materials.

6. Write a catchy title for the board.

7. Polish the words that will appear on the board. Then type them or neatly letter them.

8. Put up all the parts of the project. Be sure to include a card telling who created the board.

9. See what happens. Do people stop and look and read? If an action is requested, do they do it?

COMICS

Comics are usually meant for entertainment. But because they use pictures, they can teach many subjects.

DIRECTIONS:
1. Choose and research a topic.
2. List and describe the comic's characters—humans, animals, superheroes, etc.—and the settings.
3. Think up a plot or a series of actions. Will the comic show characters talking about the topic, or will there be an adventure, for example, two people who are magically shrunk and get to learn about how ants live.
4. Decide on the comic's length. Most comics have about six pictures—called "panels"—per page. This means that a four-page comic will have about 24 pictures.
5. Write a script for the comic. Comic scripts are usually divided into two columns. One part gives the description of what will be seen in the panel. The second part gives the words.
6. Using the script as a guide, make a pencil sketch of each panel or find an artist to sketch the pictures.
7. In pencil, print words in each panel.
8. Make any changes that are needed. Then, go over the pencil lines with pen. This is called "inking."
9. Neatly erase the pencil lines. Add color if desired.

PICTURE	WORDS
PANEL	
1. SHOW BOLT OF LIGHTNING	— —
2. SHOW WANDA THE WEATHER WOMAN	HI, I'M WANDA THE WEATHER WOMAN
3. CLOSE-UP OF WANDA	DID YOU EVER WONDER WHY IT RAINS?
4.	

CROSSWORD PUZZLES

Writing fact-filled clues for a crossword puzzle can be an unusual way to report on a topic. People trying to solve the puzzle will have fun as they learn.

DIRECTIONS:

1. After researching a topic, list important words that relate to it. For example, if the topic is "water," the word list might include *boil, freeze, steam, ice, snow, frost, soft, hard, lake, river, ocean, oxygen, tide,* and *cloud.*

2. Fit the words into a grid. This can be done by hand, though it may take some trial and error. Or the grid can be filled using a computer program, for example, "Crossword Magic" (published by L & S Computerware).

3. Number each word in the grid.

4. Draft a clue for each word across and down. Remember, the goal is for people to solve the puzzle. Make the clues challenging but not too tricky.

5. Make a blank grid. There should be empty squares where readers write in letters, and dark squares where letters may not be written.

6. On the same sheet neatly print the clues.

7. On another piece of paper, make a copy of the filled-in grid giving the answers to the puzzle.

8. Copy the puzzle.

DEBATES

In a debate, people argue about a topic while following clear rules. This activity can be a good way to help viewers understand all sides of an issue.

DIRECTIONS:
1. Choose a topic that people can argue about. Usually it will take the form of a "Yes" or "No" question, for example, "Should kids have to go to school?"
2. Set up two teams, one for the "Yes" side of the question, the other for the "No" side. Two players per team is common.
3. Agree on the rules for the debate. These should tell how long each person will speak and in what order.
4. Give each team time for research—gathering facts that support their side of the question. The facts can be written on note cards for use during the debate.
5. Have players rehearse their speeches and practice answering arguments that the other side might make.
6. Choose someone to host the debate. This person will introduce the topic and the players to the audience.
7. Ask someone else to be the timekeeper. This person will signal players shortly before their time is up.
8. If possible, videotape the debate so that the players can see and hear themselves.

Variation: After both sides have stated their cases, invite the audience to question the debaters.

REASON #5
FIND VALUABLE MINERALS

Sample Debate Questions

Animal Rights: Should animals have human rights?

Censorship: Should songs with coarse lyrics be banned?

Cigarettes: Should cigarette companies be allowed to advertise on billboards?

College: Should students be required to attend college?

Computers: Should computers be used to replace teachers?

Guns: Should a person have to get a license in order to own a gun?

Inventions: Should inventors be allowed to invent anything they like?

Language: Should everyone in the U.S. be required to speak English?

Pets: Which is a better pet—a cat or a dog?

School: Should there be year-round schools?
Should students serve on school boards?
Should students be required to wear uniforms?
Should there be homework in elementary school?

Skateboards: Should kids be allowed to ride skateboards to school?

Space Exploration: Should we spend money to go to Mars?

Sports: Are professional athletes paid too much money?

Television: Should parents limit the number of hours their children can watch TV?

Voting: Should elementary-school kids be allowed to vote?
Should all citizens be required to vote?

DISPLAYS

There is a story behind most things, and creating a mini-museum is a good way to tell it.

DIRECTIONS:
1. Choose a collection of things to research and report on. Examples include tools, baseball cards, coins, old photographs, insects, maps, parts of a computer, and models.
2. Gather interesting information, especially by talking to experts.
3. Clearly print the information on information sheets or cards. One sheet should discuss the collection as a whole and provide background facts. The other sheets should relate directly to particular objects in the display. *Hint:* Try including a few questions that make viewers think more about the presentation. For example, a display about shoes might ask: "How many pairs of shoes have you owned in your life?"
4. Decide how to organize the display. For example, a set of soda bottles might go from oldest to newest.
5. Compose an eye-catching title.
6. Lay out the objects and the information cards in a glass display case or in a large box.
7. Attach a small booklet and a pen so that viewers can give their reactions to the display.

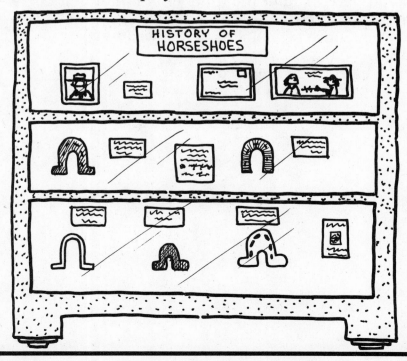

ENCYCLOPEDIA ARTICLES

An encyclopedia article is like a long dictionary entry. It defines the subject by giving lots of information.

DIRECTIONS:

1. Choose a subject that has not been written about in any encyclopedia, for example, a friend, a pet, or a statue in a neighborhood park. Another possibility is to compare two subjects found in an encyclopedia, for example, an article comparing Chicago and Los Angeles.
2. Gather information about the subject.
3. Write the article the way it would be done in a real encyclopedia. *Hint:* Start with a sentence or two that gives a definition of the subject, for example:

> Grantlin Brook is a tiny stream that flows behind houses on Beechwood Avenue.

If writing about a person, include the person's birth year in the first sentence.

> Connie Morris (born 1952) is a banker and the mother of two children.

4. Include one or more pictures. These can be drawings, photos, maps, diagrams, or charts.

Variation: Collect a number of articles into an encyclopedia volume. For example, each person in a class could write an article about a different person who lives in town or about a different place in town.

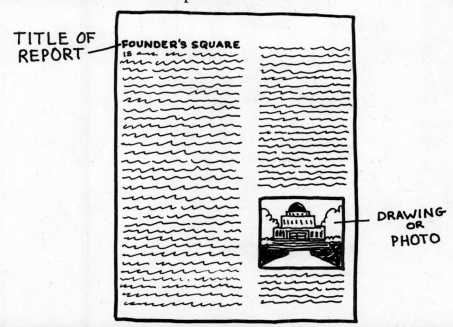

TITLE OF REPORT

FOUNDER'S SQUARE IS

DRAWING OR PHOTO

EXPERIMENTS

Sometimes the best way to teach people something is to describe an experiment in writing. Then, by following instructions, readers can learn for themselves.

DIRECTIONS:
1. Compose a question that can be answered by conducting an experiment, for example, "Does the force of a magnet go through glass as easily as paper?" *Hint:* Ideas for experiments can come by observing things firsthand or by reading about things.
2. Design an experiment that would answer the question.
3. Try the experiment.
4. After listing materials that will be used, describe the steps that other people can follow to do the experiment on their own. Use pictures to make the steps clearer.
5. Add an introduction that explains why the experiment is important.
6. Invite people who try the experiment to send the author their results and any questions that they have.

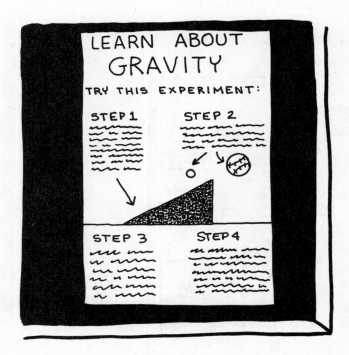

Sample Questions for Experiments

Will more people stop to pick up a nickel on a sidewalk than to pick up a penny?

Do anti-litter signs make a difference in terms of playground litter?

Does salt water take longer to freeze than plain water?

Do students learn more by studying in groups than by studying alone?

Will a toy top spin longer depending on whether it spins to the right (clockwise) or to the left (counterclockwise)?

If students watch less TV, will their schoolwork improve?

Does music affect how fast a seedling will grow?

Do cats really prefer one brand of cat food over another?

Does what a person think about before going to sleep have any influence on what the person dreams about?

FACT PARADES

Instead of waiting for people to come and get the facts, sometimes it's better to bring the facts to the people.

DIRECTIONS:
1. Choose a subject that people ought to think about, for example, the possible dangers of watching too much TV or the need to recycle glass and other materials.
2. Research the subject.
3. Choose between five and ten important facts about the subject.
4. Find people who will be willing to carry signs with facts in a parade.
5. Write each fact on a large piece of poster board. Make the letters big enough to be read from a distance. Add a picture that will catch people's eyes. *Hint:* Use bright colors for the words and pictures.
6. Attach a stick to each fact board.
7. Plan a parade route where people will be sure to notice the marchers, for example, on the school playground. Set the time.
8. Lead the parade. Be prepared to answer questions that viewers might have.

HOW-TO-DO-IT LESSONS

An important form of knowledge is *know-how*. This includes everything from being able to use a microscope to reading distances on a map. Such information can often best be presented as a step-by-step recipe.

DIRECTIONS:
1. Choose a skill, then carefully take research notes while doing the activity or while watching someone else doing it.
2. When writing up the report, begin with a list of materials that will be needed.
3. Describe each step using plenty of details. Try to imagine places where the beginner might be confused. Be sure to include safety precautions.
4. Use pictures to help clarify the steps.
5. Test the lesson by trying it with several people who don't know how to do the task.
6. Add an introduction that explains why the skill is useful to master.

Variation: Create lessons about activities that most people will never do but might like to know about. For example, a lesson might explain "How to build and equip an 1820's covered wagon" or "How to land a 747 jet."

Sample Skills

Growing Things:
crystals
flowers
herbs
potatoes

Making Things:
basket
electrical circuit
electromagnet
granola
nest
windsock

Using Tools:
barometer
compass
magnifying glass
microscope
prism
rain gauge
telescope
thermometer

INTERVIEWS

An interview is a kind of play with two characters. One character is a reporter who asks questions. The other is an expert who gives answers.

DIRECTIONS:

1. Do research on a famous person who was an expert—a scientist such as Madame Curie, a musician such as Wolfgang Amadeus Mozart, or an inventor such as Thomas Edison.

2. Using the research, write a script that includes the reporter's questions and the person's answers, for example:

> Reporter: Herr Mozart, how old were you when you started writing music?
>
> Mozart: Five years old.

3. Write a short introduction that tells who the expert is and what the interview will be about.

4. Find a partner and rehearse the script.

5. (Optional) Create a costume for the famous person to wear during the interview. For example, a pilot might wear goggles.

6. Put on the interview in front of the class. Or videotape it for later viewing.

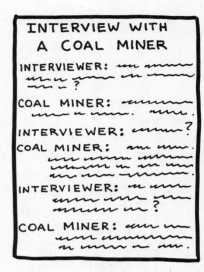

LETTERS TO THE EDITOR

One of the best ways to share information or opinions is through letters to newspapers or magazines.

DIRECTIONS:

1. Research a topic that will have importance to people who read the local newspaper. Examples include recycling, new textbooks, or household safety.

2. Check the publication's rules about letters, for example, how many words are permitted.

3. Begin the letter by clearly stating what the issue is. If the letter relates to an article published earlier, give the title and date, for example:

> "On July 8, you printed an article called 'The Ozone Disaster.' I am writing to show how everyone can help solve this problem."

4. Present the facts:

> "Students in our fourth grade classroom at Wilbur Elementary School learned that when Styrofoam cups are made, the gas hurts the atmosphere. We asked our principal to stop using these cups in the school cafeteria and the principal agreed."

5. (Optional) End by urging readers to take action, for example, by trying out an idea suggested in the letter.

6. If the letter appears in the paper, read the letters column to see if people respond. If they do, it might be a good idea to send a follow-up letter.

LOGS

To describe events, actions, and processes, try using a kind of diary called a "log."

DIRECTIONS:
1. Pick a subject in which time plays an important part, for example, digestion. The time might be seconds, minutes, hours, days, or whatever.
2. Research each important step in the process.
3. Write an interesting title for the report, for example, "There's a Carrot in Your Stomach."
4. Organize the information in terms of time and then write a few lines about each moment, for example:

    6:00 A piece of chewed carrot enters your stomach.

    6:01 Your pancreas begins to pour digestive juices into the stomach.

    7:03 The digestive juices turn the chewed carrot into a soft mass.

5. Add illustrations.
6. Share the log either in written form or orally, for example, as a choral reading.

Subjects for Logs

airline flight, from preflight check to landing

battle of Gettysburg, Little Big Horn, etc.

blood testing

building a house, skyscraper, etc.

catastrophes such as the Johnstown flood or the San Francisco 1906 earthquake

diving off a high board

drawing a cartoon or painting a picture

fixing a leaky faucet

hurricane formation

juggling

manufacturing gasoline, money, plastic, rope, steel, etc.

medical operation such as an appendectomy or heart transplant

metamorphosis of a caterpillar

rocket launch sequence

seed germinating

TV news program

MAGAZINE ARTICLES

Experts often share what they know by writing an article for a magazine.

DIRECTIONS:
1. Choose an article idea for a class or school magazine. It could be about a book or movie, pets, or a science project. *Hint:* For more ideas, read magazines in the library.
2. Study the way that magazine writers present facts. Look at the title and also the first sentences (called the "lead").
3. Do research, write the article, and add pictures if needed. Include a short note about the writer at the end of the article.
4. Send the article to the magazine.

Variation: Create a new magazine, for example, about computer news, stamp collecting, or fitness. Have classmates contribute articles.

MOBILES

Lots of things get hung up—the wash, the telephone, pictures. Why not facts?

DIRECTIONS:
1. Research a subject that has a few important parts, for example, a tree has roots, trunk, branches, and leaves.
2. Draw the parts of the subject on a large piece of cardboard.
3. Cut out the parts.
4. On each part, write important information. For example, the words on a tree's trunk might explain how the trunk carries vital fluids that keep the tree alive.
5. Tie the pieces to a metal hanger—or a few metal hangers. Adjust the parts so that the mobile is balanced.
6. Attach a title to the main string or to the hanger, and display the mobile where it can hang freely.

THE FIRST MANNED BALLOON FLIGHT

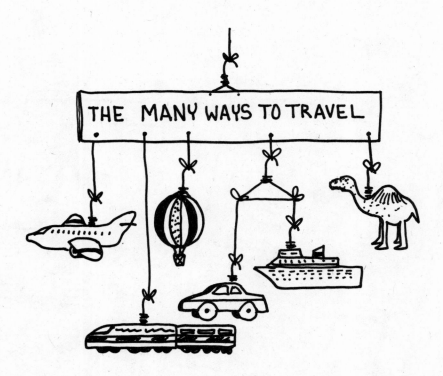

Mobile Report Topics

airplane

animal

bicycle

computer

Conestoga wagon

dollar bill

gasoline engine

gyroscope

human body or part of body, for example, the ear

hydroelectric dam

map of a country divided into provinces or states

moon

Notre Dame or another famous building

plant

province or state

skyscraper

space shuttle

state (flower, industries, resources, etc.)

submarine

NEWSPAPER FRONT PAGES

The front page is the star of any newspaper. Using large headlines and eye-grabbing pictures, it can deliver a lot of news in a few minutes.

DIRECTIONS:
1. Choose a big topic that contains a number of smaller topics. For example, "health" includes diet, exercise, sleep, and so on.
2. Research and then write an article about each topic.
3. Rank the articles in order of importance.
4. Make up a name for the newspaper in which the articles will appear. For example, a newspaper about dinosaurs might be called "The Dinosaur Daily."
5. Sketch the front page. The sketch—called a layout—should show where each article will be placed. The layout also shows where pictures (drawings or photos) will go. *Hint:* The most important story usually is located in the top right section of the page.
6. Print or type the articles on a piece of paper or poster board about the size of a regular newspaper. Draw in or paste down the pictures. Vary the size of the headlines to indicate the importance of each story.
7. If there isn't space to end an article, list the page where it would continue—if this were a real paper.
8. Display the finished page on a bulletin board.

THE DINOSAUR DAILY

PRICE: FREE

"WHERE REPTILES STILL RULE"

WHY DID DINOSAURS DIE OUT?

NEW FIND OF BRONTO BONES

TODAY'S DINOSAUR RELATIVES

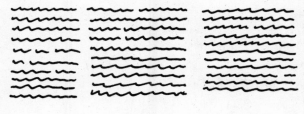

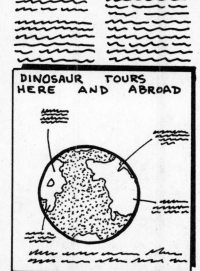

DINOSAUR TOURS HERE AND ABROAD

DINOSAUR DIETS

THE WORLD'S SMALLEST DINOSAURS

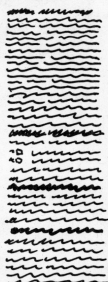

ORAL REPORTS

Probably the first oral report was given when a cave person told about being chased by a wild animal. Lots has happened since then, but the basic idea of oral reports—giving people the news—hasn't changed.

DIRECTIONS:
1. Find a topic that would be interesting to talk about.
2. Decide on the kind of oral report to give: a) just words, b) words plus a few pictures or objects used as examples, c) pictures explained by words.
3. Research the topic. If pictures or objects are to be used, collect them. Make sure that they are big enough to be seen from the back of the room. *Hint:* Pictures from books and magazines can be dramatic when made into transparencies for use on an overhead projector.
4. Prepare the speech. Even if it is not to be read, write out the words to make sure that the ideas are clear and fit the allotted time. *Hint:* Use note cards, each with a few words to remind the speaker of an important idea to cover.
5. Rehearse the speech in front of a friend. If pictures are to be used, practice showing them.
6. When giving the speech, speak clearly and look at the audience from time to time. At the end, invite questions.

Role Play Ideas

bucket talks about water conservation

carrot talks about vitamins

computer disk talks about computers

dictionary talks about words

dinosaur talks about endangered species

dollar bill talks about money

fly talks about disease

guitar talks about music

kite talks about the wind

leaf talks about photosynthesis

mailbox talks about the postal service

milk carton talks about dairy products

moon talks about space exploration

pencil talks about grammar

shoe talks about exercise

stop sign talks about safety

thermometer talks about the "greenhouse effect"

tire talks about transportation

toothbrush talks about teeth

SELF-GUIDED TOUR TAPES

Most reports are meant for people who are seated.
However, tour reports are for people on the move.

DIRECTIONS:
1. Choose a place that will interest people, for example,
the oldest house in town or a place where something
important happened.
2. Gather information about places within that place.
For example, a supermarket tour might include facts
about the dairy section, the vegetable section, and so on.
3. Write a script that tells what to see at each spot.
4. Record the script on tape.
5. Remind listeners to turn off the tape during the time
they are walking from one place to the next.
6. Create a cover for the tape box.
7. Copy the tape for the school or town library.

Variation: Make a guided tour of places that can't really
be visited, for example, the inside of the human heart or
the space shuttle. At the beginning of the tape, explain
that listeners will need to use their imaginations to "see"
the places being described.

Tour Tape Ideas

airport

bank

battleground

cemetery

city hall

classroom

college campus

courthouse

department store

Eiffel Tower

Erie Canal

Eskimo igloo

garbage dump

hospital

local landmark

moon

museum

newspaper office

police station

Pony Express switching station

post office

radio station

rose garden

school

South American Indian home

sports arena

stockbrokerage

telephone company offices

television station

train station

veterinarian's office

waterworks

zoo

SIGNS

Every place is interesting if passers-by know what to look for.

DIRECTIONS:
1. Choose a place that is worth knowing about. It could be a downtown street. Or the entire school. Or an old graveyard.
2. Get permission to put up signs telling about the place.
3. List all the interesting parts of the place and research each one.
4. For each part, write an informational sign on a piece of paper or cardboard.
5. Laminate the signs and then mount them using tape or string.
6. To help people know about the signs, send a letter to the local newspaper.

ON THIS SPOT WAS THE FIRST BUSINESS IN TOWN -- PETERSON'S HARDWARE BUILT IN 1934

TELEVISION REPORTS

These days more people get news from television programs than from newspapers and magazines. Thanks to lightweight video cameras, TV isn't limited to reporters for the major networks.

DIRECTIONS:

1. Choose an idea for a TV program. It could deal with facts, for example, a current events program. Or it could be about skills, for example, how to use the library or how to make a graph.

2. Decide what form the program should take. Choices include:

- an announcer reading a script
- an announcer interviewing an expert
- a reporter on the scene of the story
- a quiz show host asking questions
- a group of people holding a discussion
- a few actors putting on a play, for example, about an historical event

3. Gather facts about the subject and write a script for the show.

4. Create a backdrop or scenery.

5. Choose the "talent" for the show. "Talent" refers to everybody who will appear on the screen.

6. Rehearse the program and then tape it.

7. Play the show in school. Make copies available to share with families at home.

RESOURCES

Tools of the Trade

Like most workers, reporters use tools. The following sections provide pointers for getting the most out of cameras, photocopy machines, and other information devices.

COMPUTER

Tip 1. Use a computer to print large, eye-catching letters for the titles of report booklets and to type the text.

Tip 2. If the machine has a spelling checker, use it to catch spelling and typing errors. *Note:* A computer cannot catch certain kinds of mistakes, for example, using the wrong homonym in a sentence like this:

The son is 93 million miles from Earth.

For this reason, even if a report is typed on a computer that has a spelling checker, the writer must still carefully edit it.

Tip 3. Use a computer to print borders and clip art that can make pages look better.

Tip 4. Use a computer to print large letters for use on posters, banners, and other products meant to be read at a distance.

OVERHEAD PROJECTOR

Tip 1. Collect flat things that might add interest to a spoken presentation. Examples include diagrams, maps, charts, tickets, and pages from books and magazines. Most photocopy machines can copy any printed material—even photographs—onto blank transparencies.

Tip 2. Test the overheads before giving the speech. Make sure that they can be seen at the back of the room.

Tip 3. Plan what to say when showing each transparency. *Hint:* To avoid boring the audience, don't describe or read what people can easily see for themselves.

Tip 4. Practice using the overheads when rehearsing the speech. Make sure the overheads are in the right order and separated by sheets of paper. Or place each one in its own folder. Check out the machine's focus control.

Tip 5. When writing on a transparency during a speech, be sure to use washable markers. Keep a slightly damp sponge or towel handy. *Hint:* From time to time, look back at the screen to make sure the image looks right. It should be in focus and not tilted.

PHOTOCOPY MACHINE

Tip 1. Find visual things that can enrich a report. For example, the birth certificate of someone's great-great-grandmother might be of real interest in a family history book.

Tip 2. If an item is too large to fit on the page of a report, use a copy machine that can make a smaller copy. If the thing is too small to be seen clearly, use a copy machine that can make a larger copy.

Tip 3. When making copies at a copy store, be sure to collect all of the originals before leaving. Then return them to their owners for safekeeping.

Tip 4. Use the copy machine to produce report covers on heavy stock. Choose a color that is right for the subject.

STILL CAMERA

Tip 1. Before taking prints or slides, be sure to learn how the camera works. This means learning how to put in the film, aim the camera, and snap the shutter.

Tip 2. To save money, decide what to photograph before taking any pictures.

Tip 3. In most cases, move the camera as close as possible to the subject. When the subject is too far away from the camera, the photograph will usually be uninteresting.

Tip 4. When aiming the camera, check the background. Often, people or objects behind the subject can make the photo confusing.

Tip 5. Hold the camera steady the moment before clicking the shutter. Many bad pictures result from camera movement.

Tip 6. If possible, take two different shots of each image desired. Change the position and the distance.

Tip 7. Carefully select the pictures for the report. Don't include a picture just because it's there.

Tip 8. Try using borrowed pictures. For example, someone who travels a lot might have a wonderful photograph of the Eiffel Tower or of a rocket blasting off from Kennedy Space Center.

TAPE RECORDER

Tip 1. Become familiar with the recorder ahead of time. Read the instructions or ask someone to show how it works. Find out how to put in the tape, get the machine to record, play back the tape, and change the batteries. Do a short test recording to make sure everything works.

Tip 2. When recording, don't jiggle the machine. To avoid noise, it's best to set it down. Move the microphone as close as possible to the person being recorded.

Tip 3. For background music, play music from a second machine.

Tip 4. Try to make sound effects using everyday objects. For example, the sound of horses galloping can be made by clip-clopping paper cups in a pan filled with sand. Or use sound effects recordings available at many record shops.

Tip 5. When first taping an interview or program, stop after a minute or two and listen to the tape to make sure the machine is working.

Tip 6. After making a recording, label the tape and label the box it's stored in.

VIDEO CAMERA AND RECORDER

Tip 1. Become familiar with the camera before trying to tape a program. Be sure to know how to load the tape, run the machine, and change the batteries. Practice simple camera movements such as panning side to side and zooming in and out.

Tip 2. For best results, use a script. Even when taping a simple program—for example, a person showing how to repair a bicycle tire—it's best to list the actions that the camera will capture. *Hint:* Discuss the program ahead of time with the expert who will appear.

Tip 3. During the taping, hold the camera as steady as possible. Use a tripod if possible. Avoid unnecessary motions. Allow the subject to do the moving.

Tip 4. Use plenty of close-ups. For example, if the subject is showing how to tie a knot, use the zoom feature to fill the screen with the person's hands.

Tip 5. Try to avoid sounds that aren't part of the program. This may require asking people nearby to stop talking or turn off radios. Closing windows can help.

Tip 6. When the taping is finished, be sure to label the cassette and the box it will be stored in.

Managing the Report Factory

It's easy to assign a report. But easy, as most of us know, isn't necessarily best.

The following instructional sequence may take a little more time and effort than simply sending students to the library. But the results will have a lot more value over the long haul.

1. Help students learn about real-world reporting.

To excite students about report making, help them realize that reporting isn't just a school activity. To do this, have the class study out-of-school reporters, for example, those who work for newspapers or TV stations. This investigation can be done by inviting reporters to the classroom or by writing letters to them.

You might also invite a reference librarian from the town library to visit your room and talk about the kinds of adults who do research in the library.

Another option is to do a series of book reports about well-known reporters such as Edward R. Murrow.

You might also have students read and discuss nonfiction books, many of which are similar to traditional classroom reports.

Finally, invite older students to present oral reports in your classroom. See if the high school has produced any video reports which your class could view and analyze.

2. Play the role of master reporter.

Like many activities, report making can best be learned through apprenticeship. Pick a topic of wide interest and lead the class through all the steps of producing a finished report. This might involve brainstorming topics on the board, visiting the library as a group, working together on a script, and so on.

3. Link assignments to student interests.

An easy way to do this is to have students regularly write questions in their journals. Let them know that some of their journal entries can become the starting points for reports.

Try keeping a classroom journal that everyone can contribute to. This would be a place for entering questions of potential interest to everyone, for example, "What kinds of diets did famous athletes eat when they were in elementary school?"

4. Guide students as they work on their reports.

If students are to see report making as a process and not as a chore, we need to help them recognize the steps to go through. Providing them with a framework such as the Student Report Planner can help teach them lifelong work habits of value beyond the scope of writing reports.

5. Encourage students to try a variety of report forms during the course of the year.

A major theme of *Report Factory* is that our culture packages information in many ways. By sampling forms from each of the three major types of reports—oral, written, electronic—students are more likely to become interested in collecting and sharing information.

6. Find real audiences for the reports.

The easiest way to make this happen is to have older students create reports for younger students. For example, if the third grade has a yearly unit on weather, sixth graders could create a series of reports—ranging from plays to dioramas to TV specials—that would provide basic instruction.

Of course, even within the classroom, reporting can be "for real." For example, you might base a test on reports that students have given. Or you might have students give reports on subjects that the class as a whole has expressed interest in, for example, the biography of a favorite actor or local hero.

7. Involve students in the evaluation of their report.

Teaching students how to appreciate their work is a sure-fire way to increase their involvement. Of course, students need to be taught how to take stock of their projects. One way to do this is to provide them with a self-evaluation form like the one included with this section.

Student Report Planner

Name of report maker (if a group, list all participants):

_____

Subject for the report: _____

Type of report (speech, TV show, bulletin board, etc.):

_____

Date the finished report is due: _____

Main question or questions to be answered:

_____

_____

Audience for the report:

_____

Sources of information to be used (write on back if more space is needed):

_____

_____

_____

List of steps needed to complete the project:

_____

_____

_____

Self-evaluation Form

Name of report maker: _____

Title of report: _____

Type of report: _____

Date completed: _____

Brief description of the steps of making the report (write on back if more space is needed):

_____

_____

_____

Strong points about the report:

_____

_____

_____

Areas that might have been better:

_____

_____

_____

Tips for anyone else trying to make a similar report:

_____

_____

Thursday, June 4, 1987

4th-Graders' Novel History Of Bayview-Hunters Point

By Gary E. Swan

Rats, dope dealers and streets full of broken glass are all part of a revealing 104-page history of the Bayview-Hunters Point neighborhood of San Francisco written by a class of fourth-graders.

"It's the first time child authors have attempted to research and write something about their area in such detail," City Archivist Gladys Hansen said at a Main Library reception yesterday for the young authors from St. Paul of the Shipwreck School on Third Street.

The library may be choking on 70 years of accumulated books, but it will always have room for work like this, Hanson said.

"We're proud to have it. In your lifetime, it will always be here as a reference," she told the children.

The 25 beaming authors — in plaid pleated skirts and jackets — had done a lot of research on what happened years ago in the Bayview-Hunters Point area and borrowed heavily from personal experience in writing about how things are now, said their teacher, Norma Dahnken.

"They looked through old census records, they researched old newspaper articles, they interviewed people and they kept an eye on what they saw in their own neighborhood. They saw that as a mixture of good and bad," Dahnken said. "They tried to develop a concept of themselves as historians. They now see themselves as a part of history."

"At first, she didn't tell us she was going to use it in a book," said 9-year-old Rojon Kenny. "We just kept writing and writing and writing until she said, 'Some of this is very good.'"

The authors choose the chapter topics themselves."No teacher would have chosen topics like drug pushers and arsonists and broken windows," Dahnken said.

"She asked us what Hunters Point was now, and we just told her," said Cherisse Harper, age 9.

"Then she made us write paragraphs, and then write them again,"

> ### 'We're proud to have it. It will always be here as a reference,' the city archivist said

---

said Tondenisha Smith, 11. "The most fun part was talking about the royalties."

Copies of the book will be available for $5. After meeting expenses, the authors could realize a small profit.

The text is an insider's view of history, written in clear, simple sentences. The authors describe how the Mexicans and Miwok Indians were the first minorities in the neighborhood but how the Spanish census listed only white people.

They wrote about how thousand of workers were lured to Hunters Point to work on the shipyards during World War II.

"After people did a good job, the Navy just said, 'You're fired. We don't need you anymore.'" the book reads.

It is also part mystery and crime novel. One chapter chronicles the meanderings of a street person called the "Bellman" who wears "raggedy clothes and packs mud in his head."

"He also puts matches and leaves in his hair. He has batteries tangled up inside his hair," the children wrote.

The "Bellman," it turns out, was the one-time president of his high school class who drank some punch laced with the drug PCP and has never been the same.

The chapter on "bad things" about the neighborhood concludes, "Too many people are turning up dead with a hole in his or her head. Guns kill people very easily. Guns and violence are all a part of living in my neighborhood."

Yet if people look closer they can find "nice things," another chapter heading.

"Bayview-Hunters Point is nice because there are lots of trees and pretty birds. It is sometimes peaceful."

"Neighbors watch your kids when they are outside playing. People here depend on other people."

Another charming neighborhood character is an old lady who puts out milk for stray cats and always has a Band-Aid for scrapes and cuts.

"Most of the people who live in Bayview-Hunters Point are good people," one historian wrote. "They work hard and keep their houses clean and their yards clean. They want to change other people's ideas that this is a dangerous place. Only a few people do bad things, but people think the whole community is bad. I hope this will change."

©SAN FRANCISCO CHRONICLE
Reprinted by permission.